A Roadmap to Financial Freedom

Where do I start?

Chrishonda Whitlock, MPAS, PA-C

ISBN: 979-8-35094-637-6 (print)
ISBN: 979-8-35094-638-3 (eBook)

To the most important being in my life, God. Thank you for showing me there is no limit to what you can do.

To my family and friends, thank you for unwavering love and support.

To my grandparents specifically, thank you for showing me a roadmap to a life of legacy, leadership, love, and impact.

I dedicate this book to you.

"Honor the Lord with your wealth and with the best part of everything you produce."

—Proverbs 3:9 (NLT)

Table of Contents

Chrishonda Whitlock, MPAS, PA-C

Introduction

It was May of 2018, I graduated from Physician Assistant (PA) School and I had no job secured with student loan repayment scheduled to start in November of 2018. As scary as that was, when I discovered I would have to payback six figures of student loan debt in addition to the remaining debt owed on my vehicle fear struck me like never before. All the "what if's" crossed my mind. What if it takes a while to land a job? What if I don't make as much money as I expected? What if I can't afford my monthly bills? What if I can't afford to get my own apartment? These are the questions that millions face upon graduating with a degree and a mountain of student loan debt. We all respond to stress differently and my response is to create a plan and execute. That's how I'm wired and this situation was no different. I created a plan of several small steps that would lead to many big goals. I wanted a job in a medical specialty that I enjoyed but more importantly for starters, a job that yielded great financial compensation. Then, I wanted to eliminate debt, have some money in the bank, and purchase a home. Within a 5 year window, I accomplished each of these goals. While that may seem impressive considering the amount of debt I accumulated, the true victory for me is the financial freedom I now have. By executing and living by the principles explained in this book, I have a financial foundation to build wealth and be generous.

I want you to know you have what it takes to gain or regain control of your financial situation and experience financial freedom. Imagine having margin and no longer living paycheck to paycheck. Imagine having fewer monthly payments. Imagine having a savings account you feel confident about. Imagine going from renting to owning and not feeling a financial strain as a result. What if you could go to work because you want to and not because you have to? What if you could not only increase your standard of living but also increase your standard of giving? These "what if's" are much more pleasant to ponder than the ones mentioned earlier. The principles you are about to read, if consistently followed, will lead you to a financial foundation you can be proud of and build on.

Principle One

Have a plan for your money.

When people experience financial chaos, it's usually because of a lack of intentionality with their money. They try to keep track of expenses in their head and often end up wondering where their money went. A lack of attention will always cost you. You can avoid this by creating a money plan. When you create a money plan for each paycheck, before you receive it, your spending habits improve. Organization eliminates chaos. This organized plan for your money will bring structure to your financial life and help you remain disciplined in your spending. You are now telling your money what to do instead of your dollars dictating your life. Benjamin Franklin said "By failing to plan, you are preparing to fail" and these words will always be true. What I love about this quote is that if this quote is true, so is the opposite of this quote. When you plan or prepare, you are positioning yourself to succeed. You are now aware of your income and expenses and you can clearly see which areas of your finances need to be eliminated or altered. It will now be very difficult to ignore behaviors that destroy your monthly money plan. This principle eliminates guesswork each month concerning your money. After the plan is created, all you have to do is execute until the next pay period then repeat.

Principle Two

Live on less than you make.

After your money plan is set for the month, review it and make sure your living expenses are not a large percentage of your income. This percentage is one you will decide based on your financial circumstances. Usually 25-30% is a comfortable range. When your living expenses began to exceed 30% of your income, you'll probably notice how tight or restricted your budget feels. The current culture entices us to live above our means. We are convinced we need to purchase the newest car or phone, right away, only for the excitement to disappear shortly after then we are stuck with another monthly payment. Resist the urge until you are in a more comfortable financial situation. In this case, comfortable means you don't have to make a sacrifice in one area to afford another area of the budget. Make sure all necessities are prioritized first. We may not be able to get everything we want all at once but that does not mean we can't have everything we want over time. This is delayed gratification not denied gratification. To accomplish this principle, you may need to eliminate some expenses or increase your income so that your expenses are not dominating your budget. You deserve margin in your budget so you can breathe month to month. Fewer expenses always equals more income to allocate to other areas of priority or pleasure.

Principle Three

Say goodbye to debt.

There are many thoughts and opinions on how to utilize debt to build wealth. Many believe there is good debt and bad debt and as long as you have more good debt than bad with a low debt to income ratio, you can move toward building wealth. While this concept may work for some, my philosophy on debt is simple. Eliminate and avoid it. Financial guru Dave Ramsey says it best, "your most powerful wealth building tool is your income." Don't diminish your wealth building power by paying debt month after month year after year for many years to come. You work hard for your income and you should keep it and maximize it to accomplish your purpose. No matter where you land on the debt principle just remember you could be farther along, financially, if you had fewer monthly payments. Be sure any debt you have serves as a means to an end. For example, I accumulated debt, student loans, that yielded an excellent return (income) but I eliminated that debt as quickly as possible with that return. Now, I am able to avoid debt because I keep more of my income. Accumulating debt over time should never be a financial goal. There are many studies and surveys that suggest many people in America are concerned about the amount of debt they have accumulated. Forbes Advisor surveyed 3,000 Americans in 2023 concerning their finances. They report 6 out of 10 people stated they have some level of concern about their debt level. Besides the financial benefit of having less or no debt, there are also health benefits of not having to stress or worry about large amounts of debt. You'll never realize the nonfinancial effects of having debt until you say goodbye to it.

Principle Four

Build a healthy savings.

In 2023, Ramsey Solutions reported 33% of Americans have no money in savings. One thing is certain, life happens. Tragedy, loss, home repairs, and auto repairs come at unexpected times. These events may be a financial inconvenience but should not be a financial crisis. Having a healthy savings account, gives you financial assurance when these unexpected events show up in your life. How do you determine what a healthy savings looks like? This will differ from person to person but at the very least this should mean you can cover the expense of a basic emergency. This may include a battery or new tire(s) for your car, repairing the AC unit at your house, or replacing/repairing your washer/dryer. If we take it a step further, a healthy savings may also cover your monthly expenses for a certain amount of time if you lost your income suddenly. You should choose how many months of expenses you feel comfortable covering. For example, I feel comfortable with a 6 month emergency fund as an absolute minimum. So if I lose my primary income, my life can continue as currently constructed for at least the next six months. That should be enough time to figure out the next step.

Principle Five

Maximize your prime working years.

The message for this principle is simple, make money! There is a prime window of time in which you will have your greatest mental and physical sharpness. Utilize those years to make as much money as possible. Do it legally and without destroying your mental, spiritual, physical, and relational health. This principle is meant for implementation over a certain period of time. It is not sustainable to work an enormous amount of hours each week for many years. You are not a robot. Maximize the prime years of your life so you may enjoy more years than you've worked. Making more money may look like getting an extra job, pursuing a higher paying career, starting a career in general, or starting side hustles. Use your God given creativity and skillset to increase your income as much as possible in order to fund the dreams and visions that are unique to you. There are problems waiting to be solved by you!

Principle Six

Invest in retirement consistently.

At some point during the course of your working life you begin to look forward to retirement. Retirement is a period of life we dream of spending our days doing what we desire without having the demand of work obligations. Some will experience this phase of life sooner than later while others will work a certain length of time before meeting retirement requirements. No matter when you desire or plan to enter retirement, now is the time to start preparing for retirement financially. Invest in retirement accounts as early and often as possible. This may be a traditional or Roth 401k, traditional or Roth independent retirement account (IRA), or a 403b account. These are accounts you can contribute to each month and this money can be drawn out of these accounts penalty-free after the age of 59.5 years old. 401k and 403b accounts are offered through most jobs while IRAs are accounts opened by an individual through a bank or broker. When saving for retirement, the compound effect is powerful. Contribute a reasonable amount of your income consistently toward retirement and increase this amount as you improve your financial picture. It's not about the amount of money you put into retirement, it's more important to make sure you contribute something consistently for a long period of time. This principle is all about consistency which takes discipline. It's easy to think you have plenty of time because you're young or retirement seems so far away but this is far from true. Paying your future self should be a part of your monthly money plan. The elder you will thank you for preparing for the future.

Principle Seven

Pay off your house sooner than later.

For most people, a home will be their biggest life purchase. This asset is usually a large contributor to your net worth. Simply put, the sooner you eliminate your mortgage, you make a huge step toward financial wealth. Most working years are extended because mortgages are usually paid over a 15-30 year window. By making extra principal payments each month you reduce the length of your mortgage greatly which probably means your retirement age decreases. The extra payment amount is based on your financial situation. If you had no mortgage payment, how much would you really have to work? Besides the financial relief of eliminating a house payment, owning your home is a legacy accomplishment. You now own property that is a part of the generational wealth you leave to your loved ones.

Principle Eight

Return the tithe.

While the principles in this book are not listed in any particular order, I decided to present the most important principle, for me, as the last principle. If you struggle with or forget the other seven principles, I challenge you to put this principle into practice right away. As a believer in Jesus Christ, I choose to accept His challenge and obey his command to tithe. Tithing is returning the first tenth of our increase to God through the church. We don't give the tithe, we return it because it doesn't belong to us. All the money we have belongs to God and He allows us to manage it for Him. It took the first several years of my young adulthood to understand this principle and apply it. Since starting my career, I have practiced the principle of tithing and I believe it is the key to my financial increase and stability. Tithing teaches us humility and selflessness because it's hard to let go of something we are naturally attached to but God is challenging us to let it go. Letting go of the tithe shows our trust and dependency on God and it opens our hands and our heart to allow God's blessings to flow, abundantly, through us to others. This creates a spirit of generosity within us. We realize the more we honor Him with our blessings, the more He will bless others through us. If God is going to do a great work in the earth, it will have to come through His people. It's easy to convince ourselves that we don't make enough money to tithe and sometimes we may have to increase our income but we should manage our finances well enough to live off 90% of our income. I know tithing can be intimidating, scary, or even illogical to some and that's okay. Let's be clear, if you don't tithe that does not mean you are not saved or God doesn't love you or God won't bless you but it does prevent you from experiencing the abundance of blessings He has for you.

Conclusion

A principle is defined as a fundamental truth or proposition that serves as the foundation for a system of beliefs or behavior. I have grown to appreciate living by a set of principles in order to accomplish a goal and I hope your journey beyond this book will help you feel the same way. I often reflect on my financial picture just five years ago. When I graduated from PA school, I had to decide and define who I wanted to be financially. Then, I had to take steps each day that contributed to the financial life I decided. There was one driving factor that led to my execution and that same factor will lead to your ultimate success in finances and in life. The most important factor that contributes to whether or not you implement these financial principles is your reason for doing so. What is your why? Financial freedom is the goal or desired destination but why? We all want the financial stability to work and retire on our own terms but why? I believe financial freedom is the foundation upon which lasting wealth is built. I also believe financial freedom enhances our acts of generosity. So why financial freedom? Because you deserve it. Your children and grandchildren deserve it. You owe it to God and yourself to build a financial foundation that allows you to be as wealthy as you desire to be and as generous as you are called to be. These principles consistently in action will get you there. Now go create wealth and increase your generosity every step of the way!